T0095406

SHEPHERD
AMONG
WOLVES

D R .   L . H .   K E L L E Y

Order this book online at www.trafford.com
or email orders@trafford.com

Most Trafford titles are also available at major online book retailers.

Printed in the United States of America.

ISBN: 978-1-4669-3020-9 (sc)

Trafford rev. 08/02/2012

 www.trafford.com

North America & international
toll-free: 1 888 232 4444 (USA & Canada)
phone: 250 383 6864 ♦ fax: 812 355 4082

CONTENTS

CHAPTER 1

The End, Or Is It The Beginning?

As I look around my office, I realize that it has been five and a half years since I started serving behind these prison walls. As I start to reflect, I was startled by the sudden appearance of a large Hawaiian man standing in the doorway. He stands nearly six and a half feet tall, most of him muscle. As he enters my office I notice that sweat is accumulating on his brow. He doesn't bother to wipe the sweat away, allowing it to fall into his eyes. His gaze is intense, full of determination. Out of the corner of my eye, I notice that he is holding an object in his right hand. I break his gaze to get a better look at the object, which I soon identify as two sharp blades. He begins to move towards my desk. Sweat is now rolling off of my brow. He leans forward and says, "I know who you are and I know what you did." He then drops the set of blades on top of the table and begins to back away. I started to flash back to my years in prison.

He leaves the office just as suddenly as he appeared.

As my eyes focus on the shears in front of me, I realize how much of my life has changed since I first entered the prison world. Despite the passing of nearly six years, I can still vividly recall my initial introduction to the prison world. As I walked in through a set of double doors, I was met by a guard. He then notified me that I would

be given a body search. I remember feeling strange hands patting down my body to ensure that I did not have any contraband materials. They started off at the top of my head and proceeded down to my feet. This was only
the first of four body searches that I would endure throughout my first day and every day thereafter.

After the first body search, I was allowed to pass through the solid iron security door. I then entered the area that contained the prison cells. The heavy metal door closed behind me with a loud clang. I was now securely sealed in with murderers, thieves and rapists. The idea was horrifying at best. I grew nervous as I stared at the rows of bars that lay ahead of me. I'd never been in a prison before; I had no idea what to expect. Would the prisoners attempt to attack me as I walked past their cells? I took my first step and passed the first cell. I looked at the man inside, wondering what horrific crimes he had committed in order to be determined a danger to society. He looked back at me with a smile and simply said, "Hey". This was certainly not what I was expecting. As I walked the line of cells, I received many greetings. In fact, the prisoners were actually courteous. When I passed a guard, I asked him why the inmates were so friendly.

He yelled out to the other guard, "He asks why the inmates are so friendly". The other guard yelled back, "They are all kiss ups, Chap". In the coming month I found this statement to be true. The inmates started to request good behavior references from me for court.

As I thought back, I saw my arrival at the prison on my first day. I entered the front gate in my car. As I entered, I was stopped and my car was put through a complete search from my front bumper to my rear bumper. If I only knew this was the easy search. As the guard checked between my seats, under my boxes of offices supplies, and removed all my items from my trunk, he carefully checked each item with a dog. Of course the engine was checked along with the underside of the car. The complete search would last thirty (30) minutes to one hour depending on the dog and guards' break times. This would be a daily process to be looked forward to as much as a root canal. As they finished my car, I was given a space to park and was told to enter the small gate and prepare for my first full body search. This is an experience to be enjoyed and look forward to daily. After removing my wedding band and all other items, I was told to remove my jacket, shoes, and my hat. The uneasiness I felt in my stomach as the guard carefully moved his hands over my body would not go away with the coming years. I learned that if the guard was suspicious in any way he could request a strip search with the approval of the captain of the guards. After I finished a fifteen minute search of my body, I was allowed to step into the overpowering smell of cleaning fluids. I would find out later that the floors were mopped three times a day by the inmates to keep them busy. As I approached my first gate, I was overpowered by the size of the gate itself. The gate measured 7 ft. by 6 ft. wide, and it took a strong guard to move the gate. When I arrived at the gate, I was told to empty pockets and turn my pockets inside out and surrender all pens and pencils and face the nearest wall.

The whole body search was gone through for another 15 minutes, and this process was to be gone through two more times before I reached my office. In case you have not kept time, so far I have spent one and a half hours in the search process and I have not reached my door. I would have to spend another one and half hours in searches. By the time I reached the 3rd gate I just emptied my pockets and stood against the wall. The guard came over and said, "Chaplain, that's alright, you don't have to be searched. You have reached your office." I had finally reached the inner part of the prison some two hours later. As I turned in a circle to see my surroundings, I saw an open area to my left. This was the small exercise yard about 20 ft. by 20 ft. There were no flowers or grass, just dirt. To the right of me was the guard station and a long hall leading to my office. I was suddenly overpowered by a sense of helplessness realizing that it would take me at least another 30 minutes to get out of this prison, and that is without the going out searches. I was trapped in prison just like the inmates but I really was an innocent person in prison. I was able to spend one half hour in my office, then it was time for lunch. I received my meal of cooked pig and sat down with the rest of the staff and guards to eat. I had eaten three bites when I heard a scream of pain coming from the guard two chairs away. He had bitten into his pig and part of a needle had gone into the roof of his mouth. The guard was rushed to the hospital, and the whole prison was put into an immediate lockdown thinking an inmate who had prepared the meat might have put the needle into the food. The inmates were put into the main yard to be strip searched, and a full body search was started. This type of search was done with rubber gloves. It was not to protect from body sweats but body fluids.

One hour into the search process the word came down that the needle came from the farm where the pigs were raised. The farmer was called, and he said sometimes a needle breaks off inside the pig when they were injected with chemicals. So much for my first half day at my new job as the prison chaplain. I did not eat lunch that day.

CHAPTER 2

Meeting My First Inmate

The day came for me to meet my first inmate face to face. The request came from the section of the prison where they hold the worst of the inmates. These are the men who have committed the crimes of rape, child molesting and murder. It seems that even in a prison there is a sense that these crimes are not permitted. This young 24 year old male had committed the worst crime in the worst way. He had taken a 7 year old female and raped her, then to cover up his crime he strangled her and she was alive so he hung her and she was still alive so he took her to the ocean and pushed her deep into the ocean finally murdering her. So now it was time to meet him in the special holding section of the prison. As I entered the special section I asked the guard to point out this animal to me. I could not believe my eyes as I saw him for the first time. Here was the boy next door, the all American looking boy. He was about 6'2" tall and trim with blond hair cut short and one or two pimples. He appeared to be a young man ready for his first date to the prom. All this was done by this prom boy just three weeks ago. I thought, should I kill him now or wait until later. I had a small girl at home at the time around 10 years old. I continued across the room to meet with this inmate. I already did not like him. Letting him go straight to "Hell" was my first and only thought within my mind. My brain continued to race with thoughts of pure hate.

Then all the sudden I found my hand extending out to him. His hand shake was rather loose, certainly not a firm manly shake, but not a wimpy one either. He said, "You must be the new Chaplain here at the prison." Word travels fast within the inmate grapevine. I motioned for us to sit in a corner area away from the other 15 to 20 inmates. We started our conversation off with typical things like how is the weather and has Hawaii changed much in the last year. He was able to see very little sun shine within his prison bay. These men are hated even by the worst criminals within the prison. If given the chance the inmates would kill one of these unseen ones.

Even to speak of their presence to others within the prison walls was forbidden. When they were moved within the prison, if a group of inmates come within eye sight of these unseen they were immediately ordered to face the wall and close their eyes. Punishment was swift and hard by the guards if this rule was not obeyed immediately without question. This inmate really wanted to know what was happening outside. He was going to see very little sunlight after his life sentencing. As my mind kept racing on whether I should stay or go, he asked me if he could ask me a question. He then leaned close; I could smell his deodorant (Right Guard) and see that he had not shaved today nor brushed his teeth. His next words shocked me to this day five years later. He said at a whisper, "What would you do to me if I did this to your little girl?" I remember jerking back a little. Then I whispered back, "I would get a long, rusty, dull butchers knife and chop it off." He jumped back and attracted the guard's attention sitting about ten feet away. He said nothing, just motioned to the guard that this conversation was over. He next requested to see me about a week later. He still seemed self centered, withdrawn, quiet, no feeling of real guilt and was a man who feared death. The day came for my next meeting with my first inmate. As I approached the special holding, I felt some doubts as to why I should see him again. Then I remembered why I came to this prison as a Chaplain, to bring these men and women to the saving knowledge of Jesus. As I saw the inmate across the room coming toward me I thought, what does he think about at night when he is alone? Does he dwell on his crime and the girl? Suddenly he spoke, interrupting my thoughts. He said, "Hi Chaplain, I hope we can meet longer this time." We did meet longer, about forty five minutes. We talked about sports, weather, books, movies, everything but why he was there. Then as he started to leave he turned and said, "Thanks for being honest at our first meeting. That's why I still see you." Two weeks went by without hearing from my first inmate.

I met with the occasional thief, robber and drug dealer but none like him. It was like I was addicted to the fame of a murder. I felt sick then my morning mail came and his request was there. In a sick way, I felt apprehensive to meet him. Our second meeting was different in a perverted way. I look forward to this meeting. I walked into the cell block area and there he was alone in a corner area. Even in the worst inmate's area, that of rape and molesting children, he was pushed away. He had crossed the line and committed both rape of a seven year old and murdering her. I approached him and asked how he was doing. He felt depressed this time and said he was sorry for his actions last time we met. He had started the beginning of his trial. He had to remember the crime and describe it over and over again to the lawyers and police. The guilt was slowly starting to creep into his thoughts. He said he did not enjoy revisiting the crime in detail. I thought in my mind I bet the family does not enjoy thinking about their loss either.

He talked briefly concerning his religious beliefs. He had some religious background, but very little. It was mostly his mom who took him to some church. We talked about his relationship to God. He felt he had none. God was a joke of a person at best. He was located far off in a heaven. As we talked further I convinced him to listen to scripture that could change his relationship with God. I read the verses in Romans in the New Testament of the Bible called the Roman Road to belief. For the first time I saw a gleam or spark of something. There was someone home in his mind and soul. He listened to the eight verses I read without a single word.

I finished and he said nothing. He just got up and with a small change in his voice he said, "I can't stay with you and read the Bible."

The next day a guard from his area walked a request to my office from him (rarely done). He could not sleep all night the guard said. This inmate who usually sleeps could not rest at all. He had to see the Chaplain and hear more of the words from the Roman Road. When I got to him in his cell he was for the first time anxious and unnerved. He immediately came to me and asked, "I must know" in his voice. "Those verses you read to me, they have made me want more.

Why?!" I told him, "What you are feeling is conviction." He just wanted to know, how can I find some peace of mind. It is like sleeping on hot coals, I cannot stay still without being burned alive. Chaplain, give me peace inside my heart. Read some more of that Bible of yours." So I went back to the verses in Romans. As I read he said, "Not those verses. They don't calm me. I want verses that will give me real peace." I explained to him that if you don't allow the process of change (conviction) to take place these verses will not give you comfort. He yelled, "Leave now, I think your Bible is driving me to madness." He got up and left without another word.

The next morning the guard was at my door when I arrived. He had a request that I come immediately to see the inmate. The guard said, "Chaplain help this man to know Jesus so that I can rest at night." We met again for the fourth time. This time I saw a desire in his eyes and face. He finally was ready to listen with his heart and not his brain. I started to read the verses in Romans again, but this time I looked up after two verses and saw not fear but tears of joy.

The verses brought peace and a hunger for more. He spent the next two weeks pouring over the Bible studies I gave him. Then the Bible studies stopped and he requested to see me. As we met he began to shed tears. These were not the tears of joy but guilt. He told me the change in his heart as he studied God's word brought a heavy guilt. As the Holy Spirit moved over his broken soul he started for the first time feeling guilt over his crime. This guilt was so heavy he could not bear it. We talked and prayed for over an hour. He started to realize he was feeling God's forgiving him but could he forgive himself. He just kept saying, "I am guilty of the unforgivable." We talked further, but he found very little peace. As he left this time he said, "Thanks for nothing Chap. Now God forgave me but I cannot forgive myself. I now feel the real guilt that I never felt before." As the time passed into months, he started to send in the Bible studies I was sending to him. He finished the studies early and started wanting more. When his trial started we had no visits.

Inmate Number 2

I next met a man who volunteered as a new inmate to be my Chaplain's assistant. This man was in his early fifties. He seemed open minded, friendly and very emotional about his crime. He was a well respected man in his community. He was a church goer, involved in community action and loved by all he worked with. His crime was one of high emotions and passion. He came home one night and found his girlfriend in the arms of another lover. He remembers nothing of the crime. He recalls seeing the love nest then he went on a rampage. He stabbed his girlfriend twenty six times leaving the other lover untouched. He was found at the scene crying over his girlfriend being dead. He came to my office as a very intelligent, skilled man. For the first month he came in every three days for three hours and typed up necessary papers and filed.

We prayed together and read scriptures together every morning. What we did not do was talk for the first month. Then one morning he came to work and started crying. I ask him what the problem was and he said, "They played our favorite song on the radio this morning and I realized I miss my girlfriend!" He stabbed her twenty six times and she is dead and he misses her.

As we talked I realized he had been doing his Bible studies we gave out. We prayed further and he rededicated his Christian walk. He had come under the power of God's word. His thoughts of his girlfriend were real and mostly out of guilt. He found himself feeling guilt and wanting to serve as much as possible for his crime. He also felt the feeling of God's forgiveness, but unwilling to forgive himself. As his trial time came up he wanted to die if it was possible. He said same words that the others said, "Thanks Chap for the guilt." He had no guilt before rededication of his Christian life. He was given life with the possibility of parole. We met again in the big house (as the inmates refer to Halawa Prison).

Inmate number 3-Hit-Man

One day after finishing up with inmate number one, a tall muscular man approached me in the yard and asks if we could talk. He asked that I see him in the lock down area he was in and ask for him to cut my hair. Two days later I met with this man who looked very friendly, smiled a lot, and seemed helpful to others, very neat in appearance and very soft spoken. As he took out the barber kit (short scissors, clippers, comb and a long pair of scissors), he spoke softly to me."

I am in prison for killing people for money." I said, "You mean you are a hit man." "Yes" he said, "but a mob hit man for only Hawaii." He placed the scissors along my shoulders and began to trim and cut. I did not dare move. In my mind I was at a panic. I thought, a hit man cutting my hair, a hit man! I could not move, I was paralyzed to the chair. As he cut my hair he told this tale to me over a six month period meeting every two weeks.

He started as a young boy (10 years old) when he enjoyed torturing animals and insects. He felt real joy during the hurting of others. He came up young in the crime world. He ran numbers at a young age. He came up in the Hawaii mob committing theft, robbery and assaults. All these again were committed not for joy of the crime, it all involved money. He started to kill for money at a young age, possibly in his teens. He could not or would not remember his first paid hit. He remembered a feeling of no emotion after his first kill for money. He had become amoral—not feeling. It would be like expecting a rock to cry out if you step on it. The rock feels no pain, gives no pain (on its' own), and certainly would not allow other rocks to see any pains.

Saul the Hitman

Saul neither felt joy nor did he not have joy. He was doing a job. Always the job and the money. He lived a life of luxury and plenty. He ran with the rich crowd, they liked the idea of his job. He was not seen as insane or dangerous; he just had a job like they all had to do.

I met with my barber bi-weekly for my trim. He was good at cutting hair. I looked good while he was available. We talked about his job at times. He never bragged about a certain hit, it was just another job assignment. He spoke about the hits so matter of fact as if it was normal.

After two months I started to see it as his job and maybe even close to normal. His words describing a hit were, "I researched the client and his or her routines." The place was picked and he could walk up and use a silencer and shoot that hit. He could use a bomb or fool with the car to make an accident happen. He preferred to just walk up with no words and just raise the gun and shoot. He never checked the hit, it was making it personalized. This hit man related he would be more upset over the useless killing of pets. He was truly amoral. No feeling during or after his hit. His high society people stamped his job as okay, so it must be just a job.

I worked with the hitman/barber until one day six months later. He had told me that one day I would come and he would have disappeared without any way to trace his existence. I went to get my hair cut and talk through whatever he had to say. I entered the special security zone where he and the others were held. I asked to see this inmate, and the guard said, "We never had anyone by his name or description." His story came out now. "One day some men will show up and have what seems to be proper identification. They will pick him up and take him out and shoot him. Then the identification would be real and I will disappear into the witness protection program. He said, "I will try to reach you." Time went by about one and a half years and I went to get my hair cut with a coupon special at a local hair salon. It just happened I was wearing my good new chaplain prison T-shirt. The lady who started to cut my hair started talking to me. She asked if I knew Chaplain Kelley. Surprised, I said, "I am Chaplain Kelley." She leaned over and whispered, "Your friend who was your private barber said to say, "Hi" if I ever ran into you. I went for training in another state, and I was the only Hawaii hair stylist who was there. I met your friend and he gave me this coded message." I never heard from him again some four years now.

During my visit with my hit man I was still checking in with my child murderer. About one and a half years had passed and my inmate was heavy into Bible studies and helping others with their beginning studies. He started to seek some kind of forgiveness from others. He had felt no guilt until accepting Jesus as his Savior. Every night he had nightmares of his crime. His guilt was growing daily. He never felt a need to seek forgiveness for his crime. Now he had the need to seek something from the family. He did not expect a letter or information from the family. He did write to the family but no answer ever came.

Once in the main prison I again restarted my relationship with my first inmate who raped and murdered a child. He is now been in the special security unit for two years. This is a cold, sterile and remote section of the prison. He has a daily schedule of wake up at six a.m., then eat, then back in individual cell for five more hours, out one hour for lunch, back in cell until five p.m. and out for dinner. He will now have one hour for free television, reading or Bible with others. There has to be real dedication to up the one free hour for Bible study. He now prays for the little girl's family daily, no forgiveness for self.

13

CHAPTER 3

Working Within The System

As I continued to drift in my mind, I thought how it was for a Chaplain to work within the system. I first encountered the system when I received twenty requests to bless the recreation field with the inmates present. I forwarded my request to be on the field to bless it. I was told the field did not need a blessing. I wrote back to the twenty inmates informing them about my denial to bless the field. I received more requests stating this was a religious matter since ten to twelve men were injured weekly on the field. The reason it was a religious matter was there was a feeling that the field was haunted. My staff and I prayed about it and we decided that when the men went out for recreation I would get in after the last inmate. Then I would allow God to set things in motion if I just walk in the direction of the recreation field. As I stepped in line with the inmates one said, This is the wrong day, Chaplain. The guard is against us, he will not allow you through." As we walked toward the yard I heard the guard talking over the radio. There was suddenly a change of guard at the yard. He would allow me in to conduct the blessing of the field. The inmates could not believe it. The guards are never changed once placed. We proceeded to the yard and two hundred inmates, ranging from murderers to car thieves, held hands as we blessed the field. After the blessing all went well on the field. Administration admitted there was a change in the accident rates.

The next day came a request from a female inmate. She was what she called a black magic witch. She had been thrown in the prison hold for assault on a guard. Administration said I was the Chaplain and had to make sure her rights were represented. Here I was a strong Baptist minister making sure a black magic witches' rights were represented by me, the prison chaplain.

I met with the female inmate, and we discussed her case for not being thrown in the hole. Her argument was that she was only practicing her religious rights when she put a spell on a guard to be injured or he might die within two weeks. I asked her if the guard believed she could do this spell. She said the guard fully believed. Then I said this was an attempted assault on the guard.

She was guilty as charged and spent fifteen days in a solitary cell.

About a month later several requests came in that the chaplain's office builds a chapel on the prison grounds. I was told by the administration that I would have to complete four pre-requirements before a chapel could be considered to be built. These requirements seemed impossible to be completed by administration so they felt no chapel would be built. But the chapel office put out the request to thousands of prayer teams all over the country to pray for doors to be opened to the following requests: 1) Land had to be found within the prison and set aside. 2) Another organization had to go in with us. 3) A complete building had to be found and moved within the prison walls. (The building had to be free.) 4) Free transportation had to be arranged to bring the building in the prison. The chaplain's office put out that our motto was—"All things are possible through Jesus our Lord!" Within four months all the requirements were filled. 1) Land was where none seemed to exist, between two buildings. 2) The recreation program wanted to join, fulfilling the need for other programs needing land and they would co-use the buildings. 3) A complete building was found through the Department of Education. They had old buildings to move so they could put in a new building. 4) Transporting the building free seemed impossible.

But in God's time a man came in as an inmate who was high up in the unions. He became a Christian and put the word out that we need free transportation for a building (four rooms in size). We had now done what seemed impossible to the administration. We had filled all the requirements. Then administration said, "We were amazed that we had some unfound space and now we will use it. Besides, the building you found was wooden and would be eaten by termites." Of course, ignore the five wooden buildings on the prison grounds already. We were not allowed to build our chapel.

A Christmas Miracle

By the time the chapel ideal failed we were into November. A request came in from over one hundred inmates that we have a special Christmas day church service. So once again I stepped into the gap and approached administration. Once again they said, "You may have your prison wide church services if you can fulfill the following; 1) Service cannot interrupt with day to day prison schedule. 2) Find a meeting place that can hold one hundred or more inmates at a time.

This is to lessen inmate movement." There are twelve hundred inmates in prison, three hundred requested services and fifty of them were women. "3) All people in the Christmas service (singers, speakers and dancers) must be cleared one month in advance." This looked impossible again, so we put out the word to our prayer teams all over the nation. Within one week we found the visitation room and it could hold one hundred inmates with a special area for the women to be separated from the men. Then the second requirement, the clearing of all singers and speakers was done within one week of the deadline. We once again had brought our problem and request before God and it seemed done. Then the week before Christmas the administration came out and said, "Thank you for reminding us that one hundred inmates could fit in the visiting room. We have decided to do something we have not done before. Due to four hundred inmates' requests, we are going to open the visiting room on Christmas Day. You will have to move your date. You will have to fill our two requirements to do this." We ended up holding Christmas services weeks later.

Even with what seemed to be terrible defeats, God worked his perfect plan. We already had thirty church services going on weekly and with pre-approved singers and speakers. We had our Christmas service on December 25th, but instead of one service we had thirty different services throughout the prison. What a blessing to walk throughout the prison on December 25th and hear thirty different worship services going on. These were done in ten different languages. With the services held throughout the day into the night we found that instead of reaching two hundred inmates for Jesus, we touched twelve hundred inmates for Jesus that day. This is not counting the guards who heard in three different guard changes. Our motto rang true, "All things are possible through Jesus Christ." At the day's end our count was one hundred saved and hundreds rededicated their lives to Jesus. The blessings continued to roll in through the coming months. Our requests for Bibles doubled to three hundred a month. We lost count at one hundred Bible studies for individuals per week. Did our plan work? No! But our almighty God's plan did work.

CHAPTER 4

Inmates and Salvation

As I look at the five and a half years of being a Chaplain at the jail of 1400 inmates, main prison of 1600 and women prison 500 inmates, I have been asked the question, "Is their salvation real?" When I first started I was told by guards both non-Christian and Christian that I was just a tool used by inmates to gain a better face before the judges. I allowed this judgment by others to influence God's work through me in the jail. I started out thinking when these men and women accept Jesus Christ it is just fake. This frame of mind lasted through the first month of my ministry at the jail. At this time I started to see the inmates who had come to Jesus Christ witness to others in their family and fellow inmates. Lives were being changed even though I had not encouraged it or disciple those saved. God stepped in and without any of my help. He brought the Salvation to many.

A good example of inmate conversion and showing the fruit of the Spirit is a young inmate in for attempted murder. A Christian guard asked me to see him after the inmate attempted suicide by hanging. As I met with this man in his late twenties he was depressed about being in an actual jail. He had never committed a crime, just a few speeding tickets when younger. The crime was committed in a moment of anger/passion. He started to argue with his wife of five years. He said he remembers yelling and pushing her. She ended up in the hospital with a severe head injury and a broken jaw. He was awaiting trial for attempted murder/assault. As we talked, he said he woke up one morning after being in jail for three days and possibly endless nights. He felt the walls closing in and the people watching his every step. He saw the nightmare turn into real day mares. He kept seeing, living, playing and sleeping with real criminals. These men were fake murderers or one fifteen second killers. Men here within these walls were the worst of the bad boys. He felt his crime was one of an accident or at the worst a crime of extreme passion. Why did he have to spend years in a nightmare world for fifteen seconds of hate? Into this pool of a sewer you see only hopelessness and darkness. No one cares it is a society within a society of every man for himself. If you dare to look into someone's eyes it could mean a fist in your face, or worse, a gang rape. He found his eyes glued to the floor. Life was now minutes to hours to days of thoughts of possible death.

After about two weeks of this existence this man was ready for some hope. He saw me, the Chaplain, by mistake. He saw what looked like Bibles in my arms. It took two days for him to ask who I was. When we first met he admitted later he was sizing me up to see if I was real or just a fly by night Chaplain. He felt I passed his limited test. After two meetings of one hour each, he accepted Jesus Christ. His change was slow over a few weeks. Others noticed the change in his physical walk and his desire to live, even in the sewer. The guards, nurses and staff noticed the gradual change. These were the changes noticed by non-Christian people from a secular view. I asked the secular people what was it they noticed changed in this man. The list follows. His face is brighter, his walk is stronger, he carries himself with confidence, and he speaks with confidence. The changes in this one man's life were more evident as he started to do our Bible studies. As he studied and prayed and asked questions, growth was shown in his actions and words. The temper started to slow and the swear words were disappearing slowly. As we met for prayer one day he asked about his fear of sharing with others. He had already been approached by other inmates in the past two months. He told me he just shared his changes and feelings. He related to him without knowing it; he had moved way up in his growth. He was delighted to know he had already shared the Lord without realizing it. Weeks turned to months and his growth became more evident. He finished all our Bible studies and wanted to help others with their studies. He even started a four man Bible study group in his area. Only four months before, he was ready to die. I continued with his education through a local Bible College I taught at over the years. After one class he asked if I would meet with his mom. He arranged a meeting outside in a Korean Church. His mom shared how she would come to church at 5:00 am daily and pray for three hours before work seven days a week. She would return at 6:00 pm and pray for her son until midnight. She ended up doing this for ten years while he was in prison.

Another man whose life was rededicated in jail and prison is a good example of a Christian growing in prison. This man was showing Christian growth outside prison until he struck out in anger for one to two minutes. His anger came out in a martial arts kick to the man's chest. His anger burst as he was taunted and verbally abused. He kicked once and the man was dead. He had been attending some of my Bible college courses at a local college. I met up with him as he attended a Bible study I had conducted. He was depressed and feeling helpless and without hope. He knew he was guilty and was facing ten to twenty years to life. He asked to continue his studies through me from the college. To my surprise, God worked it out so I could teach him one on one. We prayed together and worked on his college courses. He grew in his faith daily. He was finally sentenced to ten to twenty years. He moved to the main prison and we continued his studies. Then one day about one year into his term he met with me and had several bruises on his face. He related how eight large men beat him on the basketball court because he asked to use the ball. The guards did not help. After the beating, lasting fifteen minutes or so, he made it to the nurse's office and they found four broken ribs, a broken nose and two broken fingers. He remembered during the beating that he thought how he could raise up easily with his martial arts back ground and beat each man to death. He had told God that he would not use his ability to harm others. God worked it so that these men found out that the man they beat up over a ball was known to walk through walls. This young man related with a great deal of pain that he had asked God to give him the opportunity to share with many inmates at once. His prayers were starting to be answered through a severe beating. The inmates that beat him could not sleep in fear of this man they had beaten might reach through the wall to kill them. They finally asked the guards to arrange a peace meeting in front of all 300 inmates in the living area. The day came for the meeting and all inmates were called outside their doors to witness a peace meeting. The guilty inmates brought candy, cigarettes and other prison things that were like money. They gathered in the middle of it all and when it came time for my Christian inmate to talk, he shared his Almighty God and Lord with 300 inmates and 15 guards. God does work in his own time. The inmates also continue through his ten years to give him the best of everything.

The Demon Possession Man

One question I get asked over and over about prison is did you see a lot of demon possession. I was asked by the prison staff to talk to a man they felt was strange even at their standards. He was in prison for ten years for two attempted murders. He had stabbed two elderly people while they walked. Then as they lay bleeding he dipped into their blood and drew satanic symbols all over their bare bodies. What caught their attention and seemed so strange was his request for a Bible of Satan. The Bible request brought me to his cell to evaluate if his request was religious in nature. I came to his cell and as I stepped in the temperature dropped what seemed five to ten degrees. As I talked with him his head did not turn a three hundred and sixty degree turn nor did he speak with a strange voice. There was something about his eyes. They were really empty. He showed me his drawing of Satan and his sketches of evil figures of death. He wanted the Bible of Satan to continue his trip into a deeper psychotic world. His religious belief seemed real. As the prison Chaplain, I could judge a religion according to the state. I did tell the psychiatrist that the Satan Bible would only feed his dangerous beliefs. He would become worse if he received the Satan Bible. The psychiatrist agreed and he was not given the satanic Bible. It was one of the only times in five years that the state and religion agreed.

One other time I knew the evidence of demon activity in the life and body of a young woman. She claimed to have practiced witch craft for twenty years. She told me she practiced white witch craft. This is a witch who only casts spells to help empower and heal others. She was in jail for fraud involving using a stolen credit card. She requested my help in a problem she was having with a black magic witch. As we talked, I felt the Holy Spirit's movement to witness to her. She listened but no response. She continued to request me for counseling. She started to yield her life to Jesus. But she refused to accept. The next day an 80 year old Japanese woman who had volunteered for years asked if she might visit the young woman, I thought how can this 80 year old do what I could not. She visited with her for two hours and the young witch accepted Christ as her Lord and savior. Then I got a scary request from her. The guard had asked that I run interference between the white witch and the black magic witch.

When I came this time at the guard's request, I looked at some marks on her back. Her flesh had been torn in such a way that only an animal could have done it. The problem was she was in complete isolation in a cell alone. As we talked, she requested that I help her pray the sinner's prayer. After her acceptance of Jesus the black magic witch tried on several occasions to spiritual attack her with demons. The new witch, now a believer in Jesus, rebuked them as the Spirit led.

CHAPTER 5

The Female Side
of Prison

In working with the female inmates, I found I needed an extra measure of patience, love and wisdom. I found the females to be more difficult to work with in all areas. The guards would see me and my female work crew and yell on the radio, "Here comes the Chaplain with his whores, prostitutes, thieves and husband beaters." While working with the female inmates, I came across an eighty year old grandmother. She was in for drug possession and selling to minors. She had eight grandchildren and all were drug sellers. When I asked about the work she headed, she said they were into drugs. She felt it was ok for them to be business people and sell drugs. She claimed they only used the drugs as a seller not a user. The kids were, after all, learning to run a business and being taught basic people skills. She felt this job of selling drugs kept the family together and working on a project. She taught her grandchildren how to survive in a horrible society. When asked about the damage they were doing to others through the drugs she felt they were meeting a community need. If they did not fill this need in a family way it would be served by hardened drug dealers. They were of course not drug dealers. The grandma even said, "Why Chaplain we take ten percent to the church monthly." I was told by her to only take one thing away from our interview and that was they were not drug dealers. They were business men and women fulfilling a community need.

My last interview with women in prison was with a sweet young little five foot three inch tall woman. She really was still a young girl of eighteen years raised by a nice Christian family. She said we as a family were church goers and tithers. Here was this sweet little girl in for murder of her six month old daughter. She was awaiting trial for drowning of her little girl. Her claim was that it was all a accident on her part. As we sat in jail she shared with me her tale of woe. She related through tears and sobbing. She said it was hard for her to share this sad, sad story. She admitted the baby had been crying a lot the two days before. She was up most of those two nights with the baby. She said on that horrible morning of the third day of some crying she was going to bathe her little girl. She remembers preparing only one or two inches of water in a baby tub. She had just sat the baby in the tub when the phone rang. She walked out of the bathroom into the living room and remembers only talking one minute and then the door bell rang.

She spent two minutes getting rid of a sales person. So a total of three minutes had gone by. She walked calmly to the bathroom. She felt something was wrong because there was no crying that had gone on and on for two days now. She continued toward the bathroom in no hurry, after all she might start crying when she showed up. So, if anything she walked slower than usual. She slowly rounded the bathroom door and some panic set in. A full one minute had to have passed since she started toward the bathroom. There was still no crying or blubbering. She felt it difficult to catch her breath. In her mind she suddenly realized there could be a problem in that "quiet" room. Her feet became light then heavy. She felt sick and unable to control her forward motion. She felt her hand on the bathroom door that was now a very quiet room. She remembers coming around the door and peering into the room. She saw the larger bath tub where she had placed her baby girl in her little tub. She could not see that tiny head. She moved another two steps and there she saw the unseen able, the unbearable scene. Her baby girl lay in two inches of water face down with no movement. She says she went into a black out at this point. She remembers next that the paramedics were reviving her. She felt she was very guilty of parent neglect but murder, no way. She certainly had not held her little girl's head down into that soapy water. She said, "I certainly did not hold her down until that loud horrible crying stopped."

In the coming weeks and months I saw a change in this young mother. We talked and read God's word weekly. After one month of meeting she prayed to accept Jesus as her Savior. She started the Bible studies immediately. About two weeks after accepting Jesus she started her trial in court. She was facing a possible twenty years to life on the murder of her daughter if convicted. As the trial went along things came out about marks on the child's back and neck consistent with her being held down. The mom said it was old marks from her abuse when she cried for two days. She tried but could not explain away the flat part of the face and skull once again consistent with force being applied to the head to hold the baby down in the tub. She stopped requesting to see us as these things came out. When it was all over and done she received twenty years with possibility of parole for manslaughter.

While working in the women's section the guards ask for blessing to be done for the entire new women's area. As I checked on what had been in the grounds where the jail for women was located, I found problems. It seems when they hung inmates in the eighteen hundreds, the hanging tree was right in the middle of the new women's section. Under the jail were possible old dungeons where inmates were tortured endlessly in the eighteen hundreds. Some inmates were even beaten to death. No wonder that there were visions of ghosts. Some walked the dorm area with ropes around their necks or they carried it. Then there was the unexplained claw marks on the females' backs only in the areas of visions of hung men. I would bless the building only to be asked back after six months of calm. I continued this pattern of blessing for the next two years that I was Chaplain.

26

CHAPTER 6

Blessings

I don't want anyone to think my five and a half years in the jail and prisons were all doom, gloom and sinking sands. There were unbelievable spiritual highs. I will try to do them justice. The highest spiritual high had to be the baptism of thirty five normal male inmates, ten women and five men from the worst section of the jail. To get to the day of baptism was a trip from the yellow brick road in Oz. Take the wooden containers to place the water in to fully place every inmate under water. The baptismal was six feet long and four feet wide and three feet deep. To get the container made was a miracle in itself. When it came to a place where we were going to consider only ten baptisms, we started trying to arrange for a wooden container. We were frustrated over not being able to have it built. Then after seeing we now had twenty five people, our Almighty God placed a carpenter's union leader in jail for a short term. I approached him, and with a letter to the judge saying he had arranged for our container, our baptismal started. The union leader had contacts at the community college carpenters school. It seems they were in need of doing a semester community project. So with in one week our container was built to our drawings. Reminder again, "That all things are possible through our mighty God."

Next was the spiritual uplifting at our Christmas services in the visitation area. There was a high attendance of two hundred forty with two services. When asked at the end of services to pray the sinner's prayer it was twenty five in the first service and twenty in the second.

Then there was the knowledge of seeing on a weekly basis the following; thirty Bible studies, twenty Christian church services, and ten one-on-ones for Christian counseling. This resulted in an average of giving out three hundred Christian Bibles every month. The last and certainly not least were the professions of faith. We approximated ten people accepted Christ in Bible study, church services and one-on-ones weekly. Conservatively, we estimated five hundred twenty men and women accepted Christ yearly. This was with an inmate population of twelve hundred to fourteen hundred with a turnover of three hundred inmates monthly.

CHAPTER 7

Chaplain To
The High

After arriving at the main prison for about one month I was told I was also the Chaplain for the High. This is where they hold the worst of the worst in prison. When an inmate talks about the bad of bad he refers to the High. Men who try to or succeed in killing a guard, other inmates and self end up at the High. When you think of Hannibal of "Silence of the Lamb" you have a small picture of the High inmates. When you enter this section it is never to tour or visit. As you drive to it you find yourself away from the body of the prison. The guards greet you with a loaded weapon in your face. Then they put you through one of five searches. These are not just pat, pat searches, they are hands up, legs spread, and up against the wall and empty all your pockets. This kind of search is done if you have a written pass from the warden and signed by the Chief of Security. You never go to High if you're shy about being touched and hands run over your entire body. After thirty to forty-five minutes you finally finish the series of five searches as you step deeper and deeper into the housing units of the High. You learn after your first visit to bring a heavy jacket the next visits. The temperature inside is always a cool fifty-five to sixty degrees. Some inmates who have lived through their stay at the High nicknamed it the deep freezer or the cold storage. When you enter the worst inmates section you will see a series of twenty solid iron doors with a one inch by six inch special glass opening.

These inmates are locked down twenty-two hours of twenty-four, and seven days a week. The two hours are used for recreation, eating and shower. Each is done individually, never meeting or seeing other inmates. The average stay here is twenty years and up. There is very little hope of rehab here or salvation of a person without a soul or heart. When they move to eat, shower or recreation they are chained with chains running from a wrist belt to the arms then down to the ankles. Chains are run between legs to limit movement.

As their Chaplain, I visited them to pray, read the Bible and just do a visible check on any bruises or cuts on their body. These inmates are forgotten by family, society, and some believe even by God. I saw an example of feelings of family about their son's imprisonment at the High. I was called to the High in the late night to bless a cell where an inmate had hung himself, a real confusion on how. I called the family the next morning. The brother answered and I informed him of his brother's death. He screamed not of sadness but of great joy. He yelled, "Hey mom, your no good son is dead!" She yelled, "There is a God after all!" I heard cheering, celebration and praising but no sadness or tears. The brother finally came back to the phone and yelled, "Chaplain, come join us in celebrating that my brother's finally dead." I asked what about the body! He said, "Dump him back where he came from—the sewer." This inmate had killed his sister, her baby and unborn child with a butcher knife. Then he sliced and diced his mom, and the rest of the family, three in-laws, with an axe. No one lived through the axe attack. One week before his death he prayed the sinner's prayer with me through a crack in the iron doors. In preparation to visit these men I was put in full body armor. This included helmet, bullet proof vest and armor down my legs. With all this on I was escorted by two guards wearing the same outfits. We entered the main circle of twenty iron doors and the guards were right behind me as I leaned to talk, pray or read the Word to inmates behind three inch iron doors. It was a scene right out of 'Silence of the Lambs.' It was like they were so evil that they might reach through the crack in the door and pull me in their cell. I wondered, would I trust me if I looked through the crack in the door! On average I could only visit two doors in three hours due to dressing in armor and restricted body movement to each cell. If this outfit does not scare the "hell" out of you I don't know what will. As I leaned to the crack on the door to talk to the inmate, one guard said, "Can you speak up Chaplain, we cannot hear you as you give counsel and prayer."

While Chaplain to the High for one year I saw five men out of twenty accept Jesus as their Savior. I met one of the five inmates on the outside doing well with family attending church.

CHAPTER 8

Learning To
Walk My Talk

The first day in the main prison I learned a valuable lesson that would follow me throughout my Chaplain work. In my office I had a staff of ten hand-picked inmates. On my first day an old, white hair inmate gave me a large snickers candy bar. This he did in front of the other office inmates. Two hours later at lunch I bragged to the head of security that I had already made friends with inmates. I told of the candy bar. I was told that I had just accepted what was equal to a one hundred dollar bill on the outside. I had to call the inmates in a meeting and make a point of giving the candy back without insulting the inmate. I learned that items like pens, pencils paper, all candies, gums and cigarettes all had a monetary value on the inmate market. This would be the first of many attempts to bribe me over the years. With each saying of "no" to each bribe, I earned the reputation of unbribeable and a man of my word. I had reached a high water mark in my career. I had earned the respect of murderers, thieves, rapists and con-artists. Some would become close friends in the future years inside prison and outside. I learned in prison your work was your bond, sometimes it was all you had to get you safely out of a bad situation. I found out how your respect and work can get you safely home. I was in a Bible study with fifteen inmates ranging from murderers to rapists (men and women). There was no guard around and the lights went out in a malfunctioning generator. The problem was that the room had no windows, just a small on in a closed door. I heard a voice in the dark say, "Chaplain, don't worry, you're the only safe man in here. You're under out protection." I heard a cry of pain and a body fell to the floor. The lights were on in two minutes, but an inmate lay on the floor with a broken leg and arm. In this case, I was as safe as a baby in his mom's arms. My word was true, and if I said it then it was gospel true. I was to experience no other close calls in the years to come. I learned early that I had to walk my talk.

There were never enough guards protecting me. I saw on one occasion that inmate trust in my word saved lives in staff and visitors. We were to have a fifteen-voice choir to sing at out Sunday service and a five piece band. The day before, an inmate came to me to be counseled and informed me instead that a hit (killing) was to take place in chapel that Sunday and a possible riot to cover it up. I informed the under-cover agent of the planned killing, and he got the information to the Chief of Security. A search was made of every inmate entering the chapel. During the search three make-shift knives were found and ten varieties of clubs. This was to be a big gang pay back and possible riot to hurt the guards. I knew the "Truth could truly set you free", but I saw inmates accept Jesus and be so over-powered by guilt for the first time over their crimes. Some men felt no remorse or guilt over horrible crimes until they became Christians. The truth for them set them on a downward path to death; for some others, they just lived in their own hell of self unforgivable sin.

After visiting the ones in the inner section of the High, these are the forgotten ones; we visit the ones that want to be forgotten. These men are in the High for their first ten to fifteen years of their sentence. These are the child molesters, child murderers and the horrible murderers. These murders would be those that required stabbing a person more than five times, or those who torched their victims to death. These men were actually hated by fellow inmates and they would be killed on sight. There is hope with time they will be forgotten and with ten years in solitary confinement helps. At least this way they have a fifty, fifty chance of not being killed in the ordinary prison population. This is the place where my first inmate was housed. The temperature was kept a standard fifty-five to sixty degrees. The guards do this to keep the inmates still most of the day. These inmates are seen as uncontrollable at best.

I was able to have Bible study with them on a weekly basis. As you enter the study/lunch room you are taken by the sterile furniture. It is all stainless steel; the chairs, tables and part of the side walls. The inmates come to the study in jackets or sweat shirts. These men hunger for human contact and words of encouragement. They are required to stay in their cell areas most of the day except for one study a day. These men come to learn as shown by their note-taking and intelligent questions. After being a Bible professor for ten years at a local college, I knew intelligent questions from just fooling around. Even here in the second part of the High you had to be selected to be here. You had to have committed a crime of murder, manslaughter, rape or molestation to enter this club. My ex-chaplain assistant was here. To be here, he had stabbed his lover sixteen times and received life with the possibility of parole.

My friend the murder/molester was here. We prayed together and talked about his growth. He related how he had read II Kings 5 and cried as he read of Naaman, the great man of valor, who had great pride and the disease of leprosy. He told me how Elisha the prophet was known to heal all diseases. This prideful man went to Elisha for a healing. Elisha did not even come out to see him. He said just go to the river Jordan and dip in it seven times to be healed. After a lot of pride leaving, the great warrior went to the Jordan and was healed after seven dips. This molester/murderer said, "I too was prideful. I was proud of my crime and felt I deserved treatment worst than this hell hole. I had leprosy of the soul. God came to me after my salvation and brought me to my place before the old rugged cross. I praise God daily for this hell hole he has honored me with for life." After three years he found himself crying beneath the old rugged cross. This cross was not smooth and pretty but sharp and raw. He found he did not have to suffer any more before his Almighty God. All the pain and blood had been shed on a lone kill twenty-five hundred years ago. This young man said through tears, "I count it a joy, Lord, I count it all a joy, my Almighty Lord Jehovah." Prison will bring the most prideful to humility. They should put over the prison doors, "Enter in pride, leave in humility or die trying." This young man had taken pride in what he had done and refused to admit he was imperfect. What change that had taken place in this young man's life! Over the past three years this child molester/murderer had yielded to the Holy Spirit.

Innocent People in Prison!

I learned after being in the prison for one month that there are no guilty people here. I met a twenty-one year old man who came to be my assistant in the prison chapel. He related his story as true but impossible to believe. Ten days before, he was a steward with the inter-island cruise ship. He was off for a few days and decided to party with some friends at a Royal Hotel. They all got drunk and high on cocaine. The party went through the night. About eight in the morning he woke up and stumbled out into the hall and walked back into the wrong room. The wrong room was being cleaned by a pretty little Thailand girl. Thinking he was in the right room he continued partying with the Thai girl cleaning the room. She fought back and did not want to party. As they fought, she fell to the floor and he ended up on top of her. She screamed for help and security found him still on top of her trying to party. He got a public defender and ended up in jail facing assault, attempted rape and kidnapping. He was now looking at forty years to life. As we talked I could see he might be half innocent. I arranged for the social worker to have him call his mom who is very rich. She arranged for an excellent attorney. He got a translator for the Thai girl, and it was found that he had been drunk and high on drugs and accidentally fell on her. He went before the judge and it was found he was only guilty of drug abuse and maybe selling it. He got six months and credit for six months already served. Not totally innocent but half maybe. During the process he had renewed his relationship with Jesus. I met him six months later and he had gone through voluntary drug rehab and was still working. He was attending church and telling his half innocent story.

35

Man Called Uncle.

I found in the power greed in prison. I found it was not necessarily the guard who was in charge. Within the inmate system you have a man called "uncle" who is the real power behind, inside, under, on top and beside the throne. Uncle was a man who was an expert at intimidating, threats beatings and verbal abuse. When I asked a former enforcer about the control factor inside a prison he said it made no difference. "In prison I am feared and waited upon. Inside, if I need a clean inmate uniform daily it was ready. If I need visitation taken care of or if I need smokes, food or sex all are easily gotten for uncle inside the prison." Uncle was also used by the guards and staff to assist in controlling the inmates. He would help in the areas of moving desirable items such as smokes, candy, paper, music books and bisexual inmates. Uncle was the same outside prison except there he moved prostitutes, drugs, and criminal activities. Outside and inside when the bad of the bad met, they kissed Uncle's ring.

CHAPTER 9

Working With
Other Religions

From day one I learned that working with a large variety of religious groups was like juggling ten wild cats while balancing a bob cat on one foot. In other words it was an impossible task. All groups wanted that special contact with the inmate and give it today. On an average week in jail, I had Bible studies going from eight in the morning to nine at night in ten different living areas. This worked out to about five Bible studies in each living area and at least two church services in each area from eight a.m. to nine p.m., and this went on seven days a week. This meant my office had to keep Bibles, Torahs, Book of Mormon, Buddhist bodies, Muslim books, all Assembly of God and Catholic materials with Bibles in at least ten different languages. In an average month we gave at least three hundred Christian Bibles. While coordinating these appointments with fifteen different religious groups, there was the ever on-going fight between Jewish and Muslim groups, or Jehovah Witness with everyone, and the rest of the group were at every point accusing the others of cheating on time or abusing the inmates. One group was caught by my volunteers having an inmate falsely signing requests for that religious group. We were lucky on this one. The inmate filled out thirty requests for religious help in her handwriting and signed each request with different names, but it was easily seen that one person had filled out all the requests. Somewhere I investigated the group and they finally admitted pressuring the girl inmate to fill out the papers. The group was suspended for six months.

The next group was reported by an inmate of trying to sneak contraband into the jail. The report came to security that a certain religious group would be sneaking contraband in three donated Bibles. On the night of the incident I was present to oversee the search. The group entered the jail and were stopped at the first check point and searched. I was hiding behind a security area to listen in to the search. It was good that I was there for the take down. The group was found to have one and five dollar bills in groups of ten in each five Bibles. They claimed it was for a donation to the chapel. At this point I stepped out and all confessed to being pressured by inmates to bring in money. They were banned permanently from jails and prisons in Hawaii. There was also the one group selling Bibles to inmates by staff and groups for unknown favors.

There was the everyday request for religious rights. There was a Jewish inmate wanting special food only prepared by Jewish hands. This was his right and my job to find a way. I did find a way via the airlines that prepares Jewish food daily for airline customers. Then there were the Muslims who wanted food at certain times during their religious festival. I found a way around security problems and they got their food on time. These were easy to fill, but on occasion came the request by Satan worshipers for their so called right for animal sacrifice. This was not allowed but the occasional virgin sacrifice was! Sure, when hell freezes over! Then the witches wanted the right to practice witch craft in the form of occasional spell casting and the drinking of blood during certain religious rites. Not allowed because blood could contain many diseases. The best request came from the American Indians. They wanted sweat lodges to be constructed so they could practice their religious rite to sweat. This sweating was done in the nude. A guard would have to be present in the sweat lodge along with a chaplain. To this day the groups are still negotiating for the process to be done, waiting security procedures. These rites and more go on seven days a week, three hundred sixty-five days a year. The worship of God, Allah, Satan, blood, animals and the occasional virgin sacrifice go on thanks to your state taxes.

CHAPTER 10

Chaplain to the County Prison

After being the Chaplain for the entry level jail, Oahu Community Correctional Center (OCCC) and to the roughest medium prison, Halawa Prison, I finally made it to the easy prison. I must have been in a dream world. Wahiawa Correctional Center was not a set back prison. Just getting to the facility was an undertaking. After leaving the freeway it was another three miles or so into the mountain area. As I approached the facility I was stopped at a ten to fifteen foot fence. I was welcomed by an armed guard. I was searched and so was my car. After the gate, there was about a half mile drive to the facilities. As I drove I could see inmates driving backhoes, tractors and other farm equipment. Inmates were walking around with pruning equipment, shears and machetes.

They were growing corn, fruit trees, lettuce, tomatoes and a variety of experimental crops. The inmates worked on the farm Monday through Friday, eight in the morning to four in the afternoon and used the harvested crops for different staff eating areas throughout Oahu. The prison also had an area known as tent city for spouse abusers only. There were five two story buildings used for alcohol and drug abusers. There was for once a chapel office and church area, with seating for fifty people.

One of my main jobs was being chaplain to the alcohol and drug abusers. There was a heavy involvement with the twelve step process of Alcoholics Anonymous (AA). My part was to be a sort of father confessor role. When the inmates reached step eight they had to write down every dirty rotten, nasty crimes they had ever done, but not gotten caught at. For the younger inmates it was five or ten papers. Then there was the occasional older inmate. His pages ran from thirty to forty pages typed. These pages were usually read to the chaplain and prayed about. These were all extremely confidential. But in the wide picture I can say these confessed crimes on a dark and stormy night can still keep me up. The range ran from cutting people up to killing the neighbor's pet cat or dog. If I gave any further details I could end up in a body bag for the medical examiner. Not all of the incidences were horrible. I can think of two inmates where there was duck involved and the other a coconut was the main character. The duck story involved an older inmate who had raised a duck from egg to adult. Most of the prison of five hundred was involved in the raising of the duck. So inmates were spouse abusers, child abusers, repeat robbers and the main father as he called himself, a second story man. They all had their input to his or her growth. You can imagine what kind of duck it was. After five years the main father got out and the warden feared for the life of the rather fat duck. So a plan was hatched to give the chaplain the "Bird". So I ended up taking this delinquent duck home to a quiet family. The duck turned out to be loud, abusive and down right mean. His true colors showed in his finest hour. My daughter had one of her teenage friends over one afternoon. The sixteen year old friend loved this beautiful, colorful duck. I remind you he had been in prison for five years with no female contact. The young girl leaned over to pick up the duck, and he focused on two lovely breasts. He leaped forward to leave his mark. He was able to leave teeth on each one. This duck was soon taken by my daughter and her friend to a quiet forgotten place on Oahu and left with a large female duck population. He will live out his life as an abusive, overbearing duck.

Now to the inmate and his coconut, when men join AA they have to find a higher power. This sixty year old inmate could not read so he did not have a written example. He understood that higher power needed to be something he could talk to and share his secrets and confess. After days of being unable to produce a higher power, he came across a coconut in a tree. He thought this must be the higher power I need. He got it out of the tree and took it to his room. In his room he gave his higher power eyes, ears, nose and mouth. For six months he talked to his higher power. Then one day this sixty year old inmate met a person who wanted to teach him how to read. He learned fast and as part of his reading was the Bible. As he read he understood and became a Christian. He realized his higher power was not the coconut but it creator, Jesus Christ. The coconut was released back into the wild from where it was found. No coconut's were harmed during this story.

CHAPTER 11

The Mind of
the Unforgiven

I would like to try to give you an inside view of a child murderer/ molester, child abuser, hit man for the mob and a murderer.

The man or woman who would dare to molest, rape, murder a child of Almighty God faces his maker alone unless saved by Jesus' blood. I met with the person over an eight month period. This person is in their late twenties and could be any race. This person had no real record with the police. He/she grew up as you or I would show no real signs of being a child rapist/murderer. As I talked with this person, he/she could have been the person next door. He/she was friendly, soft spoken, caring, clean cut and wanting other to like him/her. He/ she stalked the little girl of ten years of age. He/she saw her several times at the park or beach and wanted to talk with her to befriend her. He found her alone one day and made his move. He approached her offering her a pretty shell. He walked with her on the beach away from others view. He found himself experiencing thoughts he never had before about the little girl. He suddenly wanted her, like he would sexually want a woman. The urge overpowered him, and he grabbed the little girl and forced himself on her. She yelled and screamed. He found himself stopping her with his hands around her neck. Suddenly she no longer moved. He thought if she was found hanging maybe it would look like suicide. H found a place in the woods and hung her up. He looked at her hanging there and it was just not right. He felt maybe she should be found in the water so he now put her body in the ocean to be found. He felt no guilt or remorse because she was at fault. She yelled and tried to break free. He believed this until one day God brought him to my door in prison. He prayed and accepted Jesus as his Lord and Savior. At this time of accepting Jesus his heart was changed. He felt guilt and remorse for the first time. He saw God forgive him, but could he ever forgive himself for such a horrible crime? He was given life without the possibility of parole. He was in his twenties and had time to find out about forgiveness. I worked with him for five years throughout my time as a chaplain behind bars. He became a dedicated Bible student and a witness for the unforgivable others like himself.

God Forgave But Not Me

I have been a prison chaplain in Hawaii now for two years. I have noticed a problem with forgiveness and accepting from God and forgiving one's self. This willingness to accept Jesus as the Savior and Lord but unwilling to be forgiven seems to run among the criminals; these men and women being the murderers, child molesters, rapists. My first sign of this came with a visit with an inmate I met in my last book. In order to meet this inmate, I had to walk down a dimly lit hallway to a dark staircase of ten steps ending at a door of bars. I was stopped, searched and questioned at this point. This was the entrance to the cell block of the worst of the bad in jail. These are the men who are held for child molesting, murder and rape. I had come to see an inmate named Jim who had requested a chaplain visit. We met our first few times over a three month time span. During this time we talked about the weather, his treatment in jail and his childhood. Inmate Jim had a childhood of problems, broken home and some beatings. He was sexually molested as a child by a family member. He himself says this was no excuse for what he did. His treatment in jail was like any other child rapist and murderer would be. He was isolated with others of his kind. Even as they were moved down the hallway of the jail none could look upon them. All inmates were told and forced to face the wall as this troop of untouchable and

43

unseen ones passed by. These men had become the unclean people of a prison society. These men are protected form the other inmates for fear of death or beatings. Even the "con" community has certain ethics which can't be stepped over. One of these jail house laws is if you harm a child or woman during a crime, you will die in prison. So his treatment in jail was one of isolation. But he was given certain privileges not given to other inmates. They got uncrowded cells, one to a cell versus three to a cell in open population. He was given unlimited access to the law library with no others in the room. The ordinary inmate had very little access to the library and even then it was over crowded. And they say "crime does not pay." It pays if your crime is against children and women.

After months of meetings and prayer, this young man of twenty-two years talked about his crime. This young man had without remorse raped, beaten and hanged a female child of eight years. There was no hate for her just uncontrollable lust. When he told me of his crime in great detail, my heart stopped, my faith in mankind broke, and I could all but hold back my tears. Then I hated this shell of a human being. Just as he had walked out on me when I first mentioned the name of Jesus at out first meeting, I now returned the favor and left him sitting after he finished his tale of his crime.

After days of prayer with others he requested my return. His first question was, "Why did you leave?" I replied, "I could not take the detail of your crime." "Why?" He asked. I told him, "I felt hate and anger for you." I asked him, "Don't you feel any remorse or sorrow for the murder of this young child?" He said, "No", without any hesitation in his voice. "Do you feel a need for forgiveness?" He asked, "Who's doing the forgiving?" I answered, "God is the main forgiver." "I have no need for God or forgiveness," he replied, "I did nothing wrong in this crime."

As I left this young man, I knew God, through the Holy Spirit, would have to change this man. His heart was truly seared over as seen in Ephesians 4:17-19. Then one day some six months later and weekly talks he came under conviction (Romans 7:15-25).

This young man truly showed this verse. He was confused and uncertain about his view of having no remorse. He could see his old view as maybe true, but yet he saw through out talks that he saw another view of a need for this thing called God's forgiveness. What a battle that went on for the next three weeks, that true fight for this man's very soul. Then one rainy day with the thunder rolling through the area, this man and I went to our knees, and after hearing John 3:16 he accepted Jesus as his Lord and Savior. He became one of out greatest Bible leaders in the next three years. He was to spend fifty years to life behind bars. Even until this day, ten years later, this inmate loves and hates me. He loves me for being patient over the six months to lead him to Jesus Christ and forgiveness. But the hate lies in the forgiveness. Before forgiveness, his conscience was seared over by sin. He could not feel any remorse, sorrow or hate for his crime. Then upon accepting Jesus all scabs upon his heart were removed. The tears started to fall and seemed to never end. He saw for the first time the true nature of his terrible crime. The guilt, remorse and truth were unbelievable. He shouted, "I see chaplain, please make it go away. I am so ashamed of what I have done. I know I stand before God Almighty forgiven but I see me and I can't forgive me for any crime." The guilt is unbelievable. He said, "I thank you for leading me to Jesus but I hate you for my seeing the guilt for my terrible crime. I stand before you and God forgiven but I can't forget."

CHAPTER 12

The Funny Side
of Jail

The Inmate Too Fat

I was called to a cell by the guard to pray for an inmate stuck in a small place. The guard related the following tale. An inmate dreamed of escaping from his cell. He saw the small window covered by bullet proof plastic glass as a way out. He smuggled an iron into his cell (used for ironing his clothes) and started a month long process. He slowly started to burn off the glass. He finally got it done and pushed himself into the hole. Upon a surprise bed check the guard found him. He was stuck in the hole in the glass. It seems he had been twenty pounds lighter when he started the escape. I came in to pray at both ends as the fire department eased him out. The guard put it right, "so close, yet so fat."

The Baptism Without Water

As the prison chaplain and a Baptist minister I had the honor to baptize forty inmates behind prison bars in one sitting. We had a baptism unit made that was six and a half feet long and three feet wide. Things went pretty well until this inmate stepped up and stood in the baptism unit. He was seven feet tall and three hundred and fifty pounds. As he went under water with his knees up he immediately displaced all the water in the unit. He laid there for a minute and laughed out loud. "I might be the only baptism done today without water!"

The Crying Inmate

Over the years I had many inmate typists in my office at the prison. This forty year old man came to the prison office with excellent office skills and a wonderful Christian. One day he came into the office and turned the radio on and started to work. After about thirty minutes I saw him crying. I asked what was wrong. Through the tears he said, "They are playing our favorite song." I said, "You mean your favorite song? The lady you stabbed fifteen times killing her after catching her cheating on you?" He cried out, "That's my true love!"

The Precarious Inmate

One sunny day as I went to lunch outside the jail I heard two gunshots go off. I immediately returned inside. I was called by the guard to counsel and pray with an inmate dangling from a rather precarious place. I found the inmate hung up on the barb wire high up on the jail fence. He yelled down as he hung some ten feet off the ground, "Chaplain, for God's sake stop praying for me and find me a ladder!"

Women of the Chaplain

One of my duties was to select certain inmate women to type material for my office. As was my practice I selected women by looking at their reason for being in jail. The day came for me to walk the three women from their cells to my office. As I walked them through the halls all male inmates had to face the wall and not look upon the women. Across the radio came the message, "The Chaplain is coming down with his prostitutes, whores and thieves turn all males away!" I turned and faced the wall also and the guard yelled, "Chaplain, you don't like women! I mean, as a chap, you don't see women. . .Oh, forget it. Just face the wall."

The Not So Religious Inmate

While a prison Chaplain I was in charge of making sure all religious rights are given to the inmates. One day an inmate of the Muslim belief wanted to practice Rom-a-dom. I met with him along with the chief of security. I told him if he could tell me the dates of this Muslim celebration we would do it. He stopped and thought and said, "January fifth to the tenth." I looked at the flyer I had from the Muslim leaders and said, "Wrong! No special meal for you." It was held in March. The Muslim leaders said any good Muslim would know this one date."

The Inmate Who Talked With God

I was called one day to the mental ward to talk with an inmate who talked with God. I asked the inmate how he knew it was God and he answered, "He was announced as God." I looked away from the inmate and started to say, "Yes, yes sir, I understand. You want what and who to do what!" The inmate stopped his yelling and asked me, "Who are you talking to?" I said, "Wait, he is not through yet." I carried on like this for five minutes. Then finally he demanded I reveal my voice. I said, "I was talking with God Almighty, Jehovah, El Shaddir." He yelled out "People don't talk to God like that." I said, "That's right, and you are people." He never did this acting out again.

CHAPTER 13

Religious Rights
In Prison

As the chaplain for a 1,500 male and female jail, I was often called up to decide if a person religious rights had been violated. I was overseer of all religious groups of witches, demon worship, American Indians, Buddhist, voodoo worship, Jewish and different Americans and Far East religions. In working with the witches I had two different cases. The first one was a young white magic witch. She only did good spells for love, money, jobs and marriages. This witch became a new Christian after 25 years of witch craft. This action did not go well the black magic witch. This witch put evil spells out: death, diseases, loss of health, attacked by demons, sores over the body, just plain evilness. One week after the white witch became a Christian I received a call from the guard in her area. The guard said I would have to see this to believe it. I met the female guard and she took me to the witch's cell. She had been put into a cell by herself right by the guard station. During the middle of the night she screamed and the guard ran into her cell. She was lying on her bed and blood was coming through her clothes on her back. The female guard opened the shirt and coming down her back was bloody marks. These marks were not ordinary so I was called in to pronounce the marks as human or demon marks. I arrived and was brought in by the female guard and she raised the girl's shirt. The marks ran from in back of her neck to the lower back. The marks were round and very deep. I say it could not be human.

Even though the marks were made only three hours ago they were highly infected. The marks looked like a large bear had grappled her. I asked for a full search of all women and their living area. They had been on lock down since the discovery of the marks. The black magic witch was questioned and she said she had placed a demon attack spell on the white magic witch. I told the guards this is an attack on another inmate whether or not the guard believed it was possible. The black magic witch was put in the hole cell for dangerous inmates for two months for the attack she took credit for ordering it done by demons.

Six months later I was called in on another religious case. A man wanted a satanic bible, yes they do exist. The book contains satanic rites involving cutting up animals. Cutting heads off cats and dogs and pouring out the blood for drinking or making of spells or oils. Different organs can be used for spells and some human organs and blood are used for spells in the satanic bible. I read the inmates file before meeting him. He was in for 10-20 years for attempted murder and mutilation of two mentally retarded people. He had stabbed the couple several times not killing them and used the blood to draw pentagrams on their back and stomach. As the guard brought me to his cell I felt a strange, hair rising on the back of your neck feeling the closer we got to his cell. As the guard opens the door I saw a 6'6" Mexican man about 280 pounds. His face was drawn tight to the bone and his eyes were back into his head. His eyes were black as coal and dead looking. (No one was home in his eyes.) I stepped into his cell and I know this is impossible, but the temperature dropped to very cool. Outside the cell it was hot maybe ninety degrees, but inside it was at least sixty degrees. As I stepped in the hair was up straight on my neck and even at sixty degrees the sweat was coming off my forehead. I have felt fear before in my training in the Army, but here I felt a fear that made my skin crawl and tighten at the same time. I had in the past witnessed the bikers taken guns and knives from drug and alcohol addicts. This fear was different this time; I really felt I may not walk out of this cell in on part. My legs went to butter and locked at the same time. This all happened in about five minutes. I was told he only answered yes or no questions. When he did answer his voice was deep, deep and hollow. His voice sounded like it was coming from the bottom of an empty deep well. After ten minutes of fear I finished my talk with this man, I think I left five pounds of sweat in his cell. I knew he could not have this book, but I could not deny it on religious bases. I called the Christian psychologist. He talked with the man and found that the satanic bible would only influence his already damaged mental illness. You might ask why I could not deny him the book on religious bases. The reason is that the satanic bible would only help and increase his closeness to his leader Satan. Even though I do not believe in his religious rights to have the book, I could not say no. This way he did not find this reason out and felt it was based on religious bases for his denied use of the book. If the psychologist would not have called it harmful he could have had it and it would have been paid for him. I knew the psychologist and he would never allow him to get the satanic book.

God Is Awesome

After six months at the jail Oahu Community Correctional Center known as OCCC I felt we needed a chapel. We had 1,300 inmates in a 900 bed jail. I went to the warden and gave him my proposal in writing. His answer was that if we could; 1)Find land not being use of could be used on the OCCC ground;2)Put an existing building on it; 3)Provide for transport of said building to OCCC; 4)Find a gate big enough to fit it on the land without moving existing buildings. My God said, "All things are possible". Here was a tall order I thought even for God. I sent out the call for prayer day and night for seven days. Two day into the seven days land was found on the OCCC grounds. It was big enough for a three bedroom house even two stores. Four days the women prison in Kailua calls and say, "We have a 3 bedroom two stories on our property, we understand you need it." On the seventh day of prayer, the truckers union calls and says, "We understand you need a house moved free." Day eleven a gate that was forgotten at the back of the OCCC property was found. I went to the warden and told him of my God filling his entire request. He asked,

"Is the building wooden?" I said yes and he answered, "I can't allow it on the property because we have terrible termites." The project was stopped and I was transferred out to Halawa Prison, because I was a trouble maker. Praise God greater deeds were awaiting me at Halawa Prison.

CHAPTER 14

Inmates Who
Wanted To Die

A good example of inmate conversion and showing the fruit of the Spirit is a young inmate in for attempted murder. A Christian guard asked me to see him after the inmate attempted suicide by hanging. As I met with this man in his late twenties he was depressed about being in an actual jail. He had never committed a crime, just a few speeding tickets when younger. The crime was committed in a moment of anger/passion. He started to argue with his wife of five years. He said he remembers yelling and pushing her. She ended up in the hospital with a severe head injury and broken jaw. He was awaiting trial for attempted murder/assault. As we talked, he said he woke up one morning after being in jail for three days and possibly endless nights. He felt the walls closing in and the people watching his every step. He saw the nightmare turn into real day mares. He kept seeing, living, playing and sleeping with real criminals. These men were no fake murderers or one fifteen second killers. Men here within these walls were the worst of the bad boys. He felt his crime was one of an accident or at the worst a crime of extreme passion. Why did he have to spend years in a nightmare world for fifteen seconds of hate? Into this pool of a sewer you see only hopelessness and darkness. No one cares it is a society within a society of every man for himself. If you dare to look into someone's eyes it could mean a fist in your face, or worse, a gang rape. He found his eyes glued to the floor. Life was now minutes to hours to days of thoughts of possible death.

After about two weeks of this existence this man was ready for some hope. He saw me, the Chaplain, by mistake. He saw what looked like Bibles in my arms. It took two days for him to ask who I was. When we first met he admitted later he was sizing me up to see if I was real or just a fly by night Chaplain. He felt I passed his limited test. After two meetings of one hour each, he accepted Jesus Christ. His change was slow over a few weeks. Others noticed the change in his physical walk and his desire to live, even in the sewer. The guards, nurses and staff noticed the gradual change. These were the changes noticed by non-Christian people from a secular view. I asked the secular people what was it they noticed changed in this man. The list follows. His face is brighter, his walk is stronger, he carries himself with confidence, and he speaks with confidence. The changes in this one man's life were more evident as he started to do our Bible studies. As he studied and prayed and asked questions, growth was shown in his actions and words. The temper started to slow and the swear words were disappearing slowly. As we met for prayer one day he asked about his fear of sharing with others. He had already been approached by other inmates in the past two months. He told me he just shared his changes and feelings. He related to him without knowing it; he had moved way up in his growth. He was delighted to know he had already shared the Lord without realizing it. Weeks turned to months and his growth became more evident. He finished all our Bible studies and wanted to help others with their studies. He even started a four man Bible study group in his area. Only four months ago before, he was ready to die.

10 Seconds Of Anger = 10 Years In Prison

Another man whose life was rededicated in jail and prison is a good example of a Christian growing in prison. This man was showing Christian growth outside prison until he struck out in anger for one to two minutes. His anger came out in a martial arts kick to the man's chest. His anger burst as he was taunted and verbally abused. He kicked once and the man was dead. He had been attending some of my Bible college courses at a local college. I met up with him as he attended a Bible study I had conducted. He was depressed and feeling helpless and without hope. He knew he was guilty and was facing ten to twenty years to life. He asked to continue his studies through me from the college. To my surprise, God worked it out so I could teach him one on one. We prayed together and worked on his college courses. He grew in his faith daily. He was finally sentenced to ten to twenty years. He moved to the main prison and we continued his studies. Then one day about one year into his term he met with me and had several bruises on his face. He related how eight large men beat him on the basketball court because he asked to use the ball. The guards did not help. After the beating, lasting fifteen minutes or so, he made it to the nurse's office and they found four broken ribs, a broken nose and two broken fingers. He remembered during the beating that he thought how he could raise up easily with his martial arts background and beat each man to death. He had told God that he would not use his ability to harm others. God worked it so that these men found out that the man they beat up over a ball was known to walk through walls. This young man related with a great deal of pain that he had asked God to give him the opportunity to share with many inmates at once. His prayers were starting to be answered through a severe beating. The inmates that beat him could not sleep in fear of this man they had beaten might reach through the wall to kill them. They finally asked the guards to arrange a peace meeting in front of all 300 inmates in the living area. The day came for the meeting and all inmates were called outside their doors to witness a peace meeting. The guilty inmates brought candy, cigarettes and other prison things that were like money. They gathered in the middle of it all and when it came time for my Christian inmate to talk, he shared his Almighty God and Lord with 300 inmates and 15 guards. God does work in his own time. The inmates also continue through his ten years to give him the best of everything. God does work in a miraculous way to accomplish his will.

Money In The Bible Trick

The next group was reported by an inmate of trying to sneak contraband into the jail. The report came to security that a certain religious group would be sneaking contraband in five donated Bibles. On the night of the incident I was present to oversee the search. The group entered the jail and were stopped at the first check point and searched. I was hiding behind a security area to listen in to the search. It was good that I was there for the take down. The group was found to have one and five dollar bills in groups of ten in each five Bibles. They claimed it was for a donation to the chapel. At this point I stepped out and all confessed to being pressured by inmates to bring in money. They were banned permanently from jails and prisons in Hawaii.

CHAPTER 15

Conclusion & Summary

[from the first chapter . . . .

As I look around my office, I realize that it has been five and a half years since I started serving behind these prison walls. As I start to reflect, I was startled by the sudden appearance of a large Hawaiian man standing in the doorway. He stands nearly six and a half feet tall, most of him muscle. As he enters my office I notice that sweat is accumulating on his brow. He doesn't bother to wipe the sweat away, allowing it to fall into his eyes. His gaze is intense, full of determination. Out of the corner of my eye, I notice that he is holding an object in his right hand. I break his gaze to get a better look at the object, which I soon identify as two sharp blades. He begins to move towards my desk. Sweat is now rolling off of my brow. He leans forward and says, "I know who you are and I know what you did." He then drops the set of blades on top of the table and begins to back away. I started to flash back to my years in prison. He leaves the office just as suddenly as he appeared.]

The Beginning

At the start of this book, I was surprised by a man entering my office and saying, "I know who you are and I know what you did." That man had returned with his sharp looking cutting blades, made the same statement, but added, "I am the father of the little girl who was killed by the man you led to Christ." Then he stated, "I have come to thank you for that act; you see, I was caught on a hillside near the courthouse on Kauai with a rifle and a scope; my plan was to kill the man who had killed my little girl. I wasn't a Christian at that time so I was filled with hate and bitterness & it ran my whole life. I was caught before I could kill him and was convicted of attempted assault I because of my clean record. I was given 5 years in prison; after 1 year, I heard about a Chaplain who was leading people to Christ. I went throughout the prison trying to find out who this Chaplain was and heard a story that this Chaplain had led a child killer to believe in Jesus Christ. I was very fortunate in that I was given 2 years to serve out of the 5. While I was in prison looking for you, the Chaplain, I was led to believe in Jesus Christ as my Lord and Savior by a Prison Guard. Now my whole reason to find you had changed; instead of wanting to find you and maybe hurt you in whatever way I could, now as a changed man in Christ, I couldn't wait to find you to thank you.

My search to find you went on for a year-and-a-half, and then I was sent to Waiawa Prison to finish my last six months. While there at the prison, I heard a story about the same Chaplain who had led many people to Christ and the story still persisted that the one inmate he led was a child killer. I finally was able to find you through attending one of the bible studies held at the prison. I was determined to meet you face to face. So, one afternoon, I asked the guards where your office was. My job, as a detail-worker, was to cut the brush around the housing units; in order to do my job, I carried various small pruning scissors and large brush cutting sheers. With all of my equipment on me, I found my way to your office. I didn't knock on your door, I just walked in with all of my equipment. As I think back, it seemed a bit foolish for me to make the statement, "I know who you are and I know what you did," and you must've felt very threatened by my presence since I am a tall and large man. You probably thought I was there to assault you or worse because all I did was make my statement and drop my sheers on your desk before turning around and walking away. After about a week, I returned to your office, this time determined to let you know how my life had changed due to my stay in prison. So I finally walked into your office and with tears flowing down my face, I was finally able to finish my statement by saying—I want to thank you for leading my daughter's murderer to accept Christ because now, when I die, and when the man who killed my daughter dies, we will all celebrate together around the throne of God.

*   *   * . . . get it in that he was 6'6" & 300lbs

Appendix A.

Eph 1:7-12

7 In Him we have redemption through His blood, the forgiveness of sins, according to the riches of His grace 8 which He made to abound toward us in all wisdom and prudence, 9 having made known to us the mystery of His will, according to His good pleasure which He purposed in Himself, 10 that in the dispensation of the fullness of the times He might gather together in one all things in Christ, both which are in heaven and which are on earth—in Him. 11 In Him also we have obtained an inheritance, being predestined according to the purpose of Him who works all things according to the counsel of His will, 12 that we who first trusted in Christ should be to the praise of His glory.
NKJV

1 John 1:5-2:1

This is the message which we have heard from Him and declare to you, that God is light and in Him is no darkness at all. 6 If we say that we have fellowship with Him, and walk in darkness, we lie and do not practice the truth. 7 But if we walk in the light as He is in the light, we have fellowship with one another, and the blood of Jesus Christ His Son cleanses us from all sin.

If we say that we have no sin, we deceive ourselves, and the truth is not in us. 9 If we confess our sins, He is faithful and just to forgive us our sins and to cleanse us from all unrighteousness. 10 If we say that we have not sinned, we make Him a liar, and His word is not in us. NKJV

Eccl 7:8-10

8 The end of a thing is better than its beginning;
The patient in spirit is better than the proud in spirit.
9 Do not hasten in your spirit to be angry,
For anger rests in the bosom of fools.
10 Do not say,
"Why were the former days better than these?"
For you do not inquire wisely concerning this.
NKJV

James 1:19-25

So then, my beloved brethren, let every man be swift to hear, slow to speak, slow to wrath; 20 for the wrath of man does not produce the righteousness of God.

21 Doers—Not Hearers Only

Therefore lay aside all filthiness and overflow of wickedness, and receive with meekness the implanted word, which is able to save your souls.

22 But be doers of the word, and not hearers only, deceiving yourselves. 23 For if anyone is a hearer of the word and not a doer, he is like a man observing his natural face in a mirror; 24 for he observes himself, goes away, and immediately forgets what kind of man he was. 25 But he who looks into the perfect law of liberty and continues in it, and is not a forgetful hearer but a doer of the work, this one will be blessed in what he does.
NKJV

Acts 9:1-9

Then Saul, still breathing threats and murder against the disciples of the Lord, went to the high priest 2 and asked letters from him to the synagogues of Damascus, so that if he found any who were of the Way, whether men or women, he might bring them bound to Jerusalem.

3 As he journeyed he came near Damascus, and suddenly a light shone around him from heaven. 4 Then he fell to the ground, and heard a voice saying to him, "Saul, Saul, why are you persecuting Me?"

5 And he said, "Who are You, Lord?"

Then the Lord said, "I am Jesus, whom you are persecuting. It is hard for you to kick against the goads."

6 So he, trembling and astonished, said, "Lord, what do You want me to do?"

Then the Lord said to him, "Arise and go into the city, and you will be told what you must do."

7 And the men who journeyed with him stood speechless, hearing a voice but seeing no one. 8 Then Saul arose from the ground, and when his eyes were opened he saw no one. But they led him by the hand and brought him into Damascus. 9 And he was three days without sight, and neither ate nor drank.
NKJV

Acts 9:11-18

11 So the Lord said to him, "Arise and go to the street called Straight, and inquire at the house of Judas for one called Saul of Tarsus, for behold, he is praying. 12 And in a vision he has seen a man named

Ananias coming in and putting his hand on him, so that he might receive his sight."

13 Then Ananias answered, "Lord, I have heard from many about this man, how much harm he has done to Your saints in Jerusalem. 14 And here he has authority from the chief priests to bind all who call on Your name."

15 But the Lord said to him, "Go, for he is a chosen vessel of Mine to bear My name before Gentiles, kings, and the children of Israel. 16 For I will show him how many things he must suffer for My name's sake."

17 And Ananias went his way and entered the house; and laying his hands on him he said, "Brother Saul, the Lord Jesus, who appeared to you on the road as you came, has sent me that you may receive your sight and be filled with the Holy Spirit." 18 Immediately there fell from his eyes something like scales, and he received his sight at once; and he arose and was baptized.
NKJV

Jer 17:5-8

5 Thus says the Lord:

"Cursed is the man who trusts in man
And makes flesh his strength,
Whose heart departs from the Lord.
6 For he shall be like a shrub in the desert,
And shall not see when good comes,
But shall inhabit the parched places in the wilderness,
In a salt land which is not inhabited.

7 "Blessed is the man who trusts in the Lord,
And whose hope is the Lord.
8 For he shall be like a tree planted by the waters,
Which spreads out its roots by the river,

And will not fear when heat comes;
But its leaf will be green,
And will not be anxious in the year of drought,
Nor will cease from yielding fruit.
NKJV

Jer 17:5-8

5 Thus says the Lord:

"Cursed is the man who trusts in man
And makes flesh his strength,
Whose heart departs from the Lord.
6 For he shall be like a shrub in the desert,
And shall not see when good comes,
But shall inhabit the parched places in the wilderness,
In a salt land which is not inhabited.

7 "Blessed is the man who trusts in the Lord,
And whose hope is the Lord.
8 For he shall be like a tree planted by the waters,
Which spreads out its roots by the river,
And will not fear when heat comes;
But its leaf will be green,
And will not be anxious in the year of drought,
Nor will cease from yielding fruit.
NKJV

Ps 27:1-7 he Lord is my light and my salvation;Whom shall I fear?The Lord is the strength of my life;Of whom shall I be afraid? 2 When the wicked came against meTo eat up my flesh,My enemies and foes,They stumbled and fell. 3 Though an army may encamp against me,My heart shall not fear;Though war may rise against me,In this I will be confident.

4 One thing I have desired of the Lord,That will I seek:That I may dwell in the house of the LordAll the days of my life,To behold the

beauty of the Lord,And to inquire in His temple. 5 For in the time of troubleHe shall hide me in His pavilion;In the secret place of His tabernacleHe shall hide me;He shall set me high upon a rock.

6 And now my head shall be lifted up above my enemies all around me;Therefore I will offer sacrifices of joy in His tabernacle;I will sing, yes, I will sing praises to the Lord.
7 Hear,
NKJV

Ps 27:1-7 he Lord is my light and my salvation;Whom shall I fear?The Lord is the strength of my life;Of whom shall I be afraid? 2 When the wicked came against meTo eat up my flesh,My enemies and foes,They stumbled and fell. 3 Though an army may encamp against me,My heart shall not fear;Though war may rise against me,In this I will be confident.

4 One thing I have desired of the Lord,That will I seek:That I may dwell in the house of the LordAll the days of my life,To behold the beauty of the Lord,And to inquire in His temple. 5 For in the time of troubleHe shall hide me in His pavilion;In the secret place of His tabernacleHe shall hide me;He shall set me high upon a rock.

6 And now my head shall be lifted up above my enemies all around me;Therefore I will offer sacrifices of joy in His tabernacle;I will sing, yes, I will sing praises to the Lord.
7 Hear,
NKJV

Isa 12:1-3

And in that day you will say:

"O Lord, I will praise You;
Though You were angry with me,
Your anger is turned away, and You comfort me.
2 Behold, God is my salvation,

I will trust and not be afraid;
'For Yah, the Lord, is my strength and song;
He also has become my salvation.'"

3 Therefore with joy you will draw water
From the wells of salvation.
NKJV

Rom 10:9-13
9 that if you confess with your mouth the Lord Jesus and believe in
your heart that God has raised Him from the dead, you will be saved.
10 For with the heart one believes unto righteousness, and with the
mouth confession is made unto salvation. 11 For the Scripture says,
"Whoever believes on Him will not be put to shame." 12 For there is
no distinction between Jew and Greek, for the same Lord over all is
rich to all who call upon Him. 13 For "whoever calls on the name of
the Lord shall be saved."
NKJV

Matt 8:28-9:1

28 Two Demon-Possessed Men Healed

(Mark 5:1-20; Luke 8:26-39)

When He had come to the other side, to the country of the Gergesenes,
there met Him two demon-possessed men, coming out of the tombs,
exceedingly fierce, so that no one could pass that way. 29 And
suddenly they cried out, saying, "What have we to do with You,
Jesus, You Son of God? Have You come here to torment us before
the time?"

30 Now a good way off from them there was a herd of many swine
feeding. 31 So the demons begged Him, saying, "If You cast us out,
permit us to go away into the herd of swine."

32 And He said to them, "Go." So when they had come out, they went into the herd of swine. And suddenly the whole herd of swine ran violently down the steep place into the sea, and perished in the water.

33 Then those who kept them fled; and they went away into the city and told everything, including what had happened to the demon-possessed men. 34 And behold, the whole city came out to meet Jesus. And when they saw Him, they begged Him to depart from their region.

NKJV

God Goes Before Us—II Chronicles 20

2 Chron 20:1-26

It happened after this that the people of Moab with the people of Ammon, and others with them besides the Ammonites, came to battle against Jehoshaphat. 2 Then some came and told Jehoshaphat, saying, "A great multitude is coming against you from beyond the sea, from Syria; and they are in Hazazon Tamar" (which is En Gedi). 3 And Jehoshaphat feared, and set himself to seek the Lord, and proclaimed a fast throughout all Judah. 4 So Judah gathered together to ask help from the Lord; and from all the cities of Judah they came to seek the Lord. 5 Then Jehoshaphat stood in the assembly of Judah and Jerusalem, in the house of the Lord, before the new court, 6 and said: "O Lord God of our fathers, are You not God in heaven, and do You not rule over all the kingdoms of the nations, and in Your hand is there not power and might, so that no one is able to withstand You? 7 Are You not our God, who drove out the inhabitants of this land before Your people Israel, and gave it to the descendants of Abraham Your friend forever? 8 And they dwell in it, and have built You a sanctuary in it for Your name, saying, 9'If disaster comes upon us—sword, judgment, pestilence, or famine—we will stand before this temple and in Your presence (for Your name is in this temple), and cry out to You in our affliction, and You will hear and save.' 10 And now, here are the people of Ammon, Moab, and Mount Seir—whom You would not let Israel invade when they came out of the land of Egypt, but they turned from them and did not destroy them—11 here they are, rewarding us by coming to throw us out of Your possession which You have given us to inherit. 12 O our God, will You not judge them? For we have no power against this great multitude that is coming against us; nor do we know what to do, but our eyes are upon You."

13 Now all Judah, with their little ones, their wives, and their children, stood before the Lord. 14 Then the Spirit of the Lord came upon Jahaziel the son of Zechariah, the son of Benaiah, the son of Jeiel, the son of Mattaniah, a Levite of the sons of Asaph, in the midst of the assembly. 15 And he said, "Listen, all you of Judah and you inhabitants of Jerusalem, and you, King Jehoshaphat! Thus says the Lord to you:'Do not be afraid nor dismayed because of this great multitude, for the battle is not yours, but God's. 16 Tomorrow go down against them. They will surely come up by the Ascent of Ziz, and you will find them at the end of the brook before the Wilderness of Jeruel. 17 You will not need to fight in this battle. Position yourselves, stand still and see the salvation of the Lord, who is with you, O Judah and Jerusalem!' Do not fear or be dismayed; tomorrow go out against them, for the Lord is with you."

18 And Jehoshaphat bowed his head with his face to the ground, and all Judah and the inhabitants of Jerusalem bowed before the Lord, worshiping the Lord. 19 Then the Levites of the children of the Kohathites and of the children of the Korahites stood up to praise the Lord God of Israel with voices loud and high.

20 So they rose early in the morning and went out into the Wilderness of Tekoa; and as they went out, Jehoshaphat stood and said, "Hear me, O Judah and you inhabitants of Jerusalem: Believe in the Lord your God, and you shall be established; believe His prophets, and you shall prosper." 21 And when he had consulted with the people, he appointed those who should sing to the Lord, and who should

praise the beauty of holiness, as they went out before the army and were saying:

"Praise the Lord,For His mercy endures forever."
22 Now when they began to sing and to praise, the Lord set ambushes against the people of Ammon, Moab, and Mount Seir, who had come against Judah; and they were defeated. 23 For the people of Ammon and Moab stood up against the inhabitants of Mount Seir to utterly kill and destroy them. And when they had made an end of the inhabitants of Seir, they helped to destroy one another.

24 So when Judah came to a place overlooking the wilderness, they looked toward the multitude; and there were their dead bodies, fallen on the earth. No one had escaped.
25 When Jehoshaphat and his people came to take away their spoil, they found among them an abundance of valuables on the dead bodies, and precious jewelry, which they stripped off for themselves, more than they could carry away; and they were three days gathering the spoil because there was so much. 2
NKJV

Rom 6:1-11

6:1 Dead to Sin, Alive to God

What shall we say then? Shall we continue in sin that grace may abound? 2 Certainly not! How shall we who died to sin live any longer in it? 3 Or do you not know that as many of us as were baptized into Christ Jesus were baptized into His death? 4 Therefore we were buried with Him through baptism into death, that just as Christ was raised from the dead by the glory of the Father, even so we also should walk in newness of life.

5 For if we have been united together in the likeness of His death, certainly we also shall be in the likeness of His resurrection, 6 knowing this, that our old man was crucified with Him, that the body of sin might be done away with, that we should no longer be slaves of

sin. 7 For he who has died has been freed from sin. 8 Now if we died with Christ, we believe that we shall also live with Him, 9 knowing that Christ, having been raised from the dead, dies no more. Death no longer has dominion over Him. 10 For the death that He died, He died to sin once for all; but the life that He lives, He lives to God. 11 Likewise you also, reckon yourselves to be dead indeed to sin, but alive to God in Christ Jesus our Lord.
NKJV

2 Cor 5:1-8

For we know that if our earthly house, this tent, is destroyed, we have a building from God, a house not made with hands, eternal in the heavens. 2 For in this we groan, earnestly desiring to be clothed with our habitation which is from heaven, 3 if indeed, having been clothed, we shall not be found naked. 4 For we who are in this tent groan, being burdened, not because we want to be unclothed, but further clothed, that mortality may be swallowed up by life. 5 Now He who has prepared us for this very thing is God, who also has given us the Spirit as a guarantee.

6 So we are always confident, knowing that while we are at home in the body we are absent from the Lord. 7 For we walk by faith, not by sight. 8 We are confident, yes, well pleased rather to be absent from the body and to be present with the Lord.
NKJV

Matt 10:21-26

21 "Now brother will deliver up brother to death, and a father his child; and children will rise up against parents and cause them to be put to death. 22 And you will be hated by all for My name's sake. But he who endures to the end will be saved. 23 When they persecute you in this city, flee to another. For assuredly, I say to you, you will not have gone through the cities of Israel before the Son of Man comes.

24 "A disciple is not above his teacher, nor a servant above his master. 25 It is enough for a disciple that he be like his teacher, and a servant like his master. If they have called the master of the house Beelzebub, how much more will they call those of his household! 26 Therefore do not fear them. For there is nothing covered that will not be revealed, and hidden that will not be known.
NKJV

Matt 6:14-15

14 "For if you forgive men their trespasses, your heavenly Father will also forgive you. 15 But if you do not forgive men their trespasses, neither will your Father forgive your trespasses.
NKJV